The Boat-Maker's Art

The Boat-Maker's Art

Poems by

Shaheen Dil

© 2024 Shaheen Dil. All rights reserved.
This material may not be reproduced in any form, published,
reprinted, recorded, performed, broadcast,
rewritten, or redistributed without
the explicit permission of Shaheen Dil.
All such actions are strictly prohibited by law.

Cover design by Shay Culligan
Cover image by David Muenzer
Author photo by JMKL Creative

ISBN: 978-1-63980-493-1

Kelsay Books
502 South 1040 East, A-119
American Fork, Utah 84003
Kelsaybooks.com

For Clark,
who makes all of this possible

Acknowledgments

The Boat-Maker's Art came to life with the support and encouragement of many people. Let me start with a heartfelt "thank you" to my friend, the Bulgarian-American poet Lyubomir Nikolov, who read and critiqued every poem in multiple versions, and to Michael Wurster, the dean of Pittsburgh poetry, who nurtured my poetic growth for many years. Fellow participants in poetry workshops—the Pittsburgh Poetry Exchange, the DVP/US1 Poets, and the Porch Poets—commented on earlier versions of many of these poems: Timons Esaias, Arlene Wiener, Ziggy Edwards, Alyssa Sineni, Roberta Hatcher, Judy Robinson, Stuart Shephard, Joan Bauer, and Judith Dorian, among others. Last, but not least, I want to thank my family: my Goethe-manic husband, Clark Muenzer, my artist son David Muenzer, and my physician/aerialist daughter Maya Muenzer, whose support keeps me going.

A number of these poems were first published in the following journals, some in slightly different forms:

CALYX Journal: "August," "Aubade"
A Critique of the Gods: "Prayer"
The Golden Streetcar: "My Mother's Garden"
Gyroscope Review: "The Boat-Maker's Art"
The Last Stanza Poetry Journal: "The Opposite of Telescope"
Main Street Rag: "Driving on the PA Turnpike"
Masque & Spectacle: "Sampsonia at Night"
The Orchards Poetry Journal: "Post Cataracts"
Passager: "River at Night"
Rune: "The First Snowfall"
Stripes Literary Magazine: "Chrysolite," "Dust"
Uppagus: "Wind from the 45th Floor"
US1 Worksheets: "Horology," "Turning Point"
Vox Populi: "Properties of the Number Nineteen"

Contents

I. Bhajan

The Boat-Maker's Art	15
Prayer	19
Bhajan	20
Morning Yoga	21
Karimpur	22
The Opposite of Telescope	23
Along the Canal	25
Portent	26
Dancing	27
Chrysolite	28
Finding the Center	29
Colors	30
River at Night	31

II. The Properties of Time

Horology	35
Inkling	36
Properties of Time	40
Properties of the Number Nineteen	41
A Rumor of Blue	43
Rose	44
Turning Point	45
Backward Look	46
Coffee Mugs	47
Walking in the Homewood Cemetery	48
Rails to Trails	49
Sports Day	52
Bolinas	53
Kennywood Days	54
My Mother's Garden	55

For Ruth	56
Dinner at El Vez	57
How the West was Won	59
Sampsonia at Night	60
Nefertiti's Daughters	61

III. Mad Birds and Shadows

Eating a Blood Orange in the Morning	67
August	68
Wind from the 45th Floor	69
Pink Moon	70
A Hint of Pink	71
Promises Mailboxes Make	72
Departure	73
The First Snowfall	74
Dust	75
Day's End	76
Nightscape	77
What Happened	78
Driving on the PA Turnpike	79
Aubade	80
Riptide	81
If Then	82
Memory	83
Breakable Things	84
Beguiled	85
Nights	86
After Rilke	87
The Globe	88
Beaches	89
Properties of Green	90
After Cataracts	94
The Red Thread	97

I. Bhajan

"I sell mirrors in the city of the blind."
—Kabir

"She would make both dance, she thought, fist to fist—
And she would glide, so smooth, along the tightrope,
She thought she could do absolutely anything at all.
Only once in your life will the rope shiver."
—Nabaneeta Dev Sen

The Boat-Maker's Art

I.

I watched the boat as it was built—
the shine of wood,
the decadent lines of it,
hand-polished surfaces gleaming,
sleek, tempting,
half-done and up on trestles,
looking for all the world as if it wanted to leap into the water,
sails unfurled,
bow springing above the waves,
stern slicing through sprays of spume.

The boat-maker's hands gentle,
sanding the sides.

Unaware of the camera's gaze,
voyeurs peeping through lenses
trained on his hands,
he worked while we watched,
absorbed and unconcerned,
secure in his place as master-builder,
a yacht with sails,
no fiberglass, no engine.

II.

I imagine Galatea being chiseled
with that precision—
the maker chipping at her perfect form—
fusing design to desire.

III.

> *On the Ganges delta, crisscrossed by rivers,*
> *fishermen abandoned wooden sailing boats and dugouts*
> *(designs over 3,000 years old).*

IV.

In Narsingdi Ghat boat-builders stand
ankle-deep in mud,
lunghis hitched up around their hips,
building power boats and motorized dinghies
using traditional tools
    (hammer, nail, chisel, wood planer, bow saw, lathe)
and mass-produced engines
    (cheap, efficient),
the fire of focus in their eyes.

Their hands gentle,
the hull bending to their touch.

These boats are both love and livelihood—
they are to fish,
to eat,
to live,
to race.

V.

*Not to be confused with the ship-building industry
in the dockyards at Buriganga or Chittagong,
vying with China, Japan, and South Korea
to export ocean-going vessels and warships.*

*Back to historic pre-eminence—
in 1770, Bengal built 223,250 tons of ocean-going ships—
compared to just 23,061 in the restive American colonies.*

VI.

The mazhi launches his finished nauka,
beating back thick fronds of lotus leaves clustering the edges
with his long pole,
slicing through pink blossoms,
the boat glides into the river,
phut phut of the engine starts,
black fumes trailing behind.

Nets cast into the deep of the inlet,
marked by buoys.
He will return before dawn the next day
to harvest his catch.

VII.

The *Apache Star,*
a fiberglass monstrosity,
dove into the water like a red rocket,
engines roaring,
achieved speeds of 115 knots—
set a world record from Miami to Havana
and back.

VIII.

Charon lifts up his oar,
pushes off from the edge.

The ripple of black water makes no sound.

Prayer

I send words into dense air—
making prayer not on knees but haunches,

head turning this way and that, as if Gadal turned his wands
into guidesticks—the thousand-stitched prayer mat

burning red and blue in the unspeakable dark:
Aten, Adonai, Allah—give it breath—

by whatever words we choose to sing, sending hope into the abyss
as if despair could be atoned and dusk repaired to what it was

before Eve plucked the crimson fruit and plunged
(we are told) into never-ending night.

I drop words into solitude, break surface without a splash,
insult to the water, oscillation—

could there be another way to speak?
The way Adam first spoke to Eve,

wordless, before language, patterns we cannot break—
or was it Eve who needed to define

what she saw—the world before she knew it—
standing there, before her, a reflection something like herself,

oddly similar, but also, alluring difference—
before she learned disguise, the red confusion of words,

before sound, startling like the first flute,
sending the first prayer to a silent God?

Bhajan

Raindrops keep changing back and forth—
in one instant slow snowflakes falling one by luminous one,

turning into gray droplets lifted by icy gusts
slashing windowpanes, then back to smoky patterns in air.

If only we were there, filtering the sound of flowing wind,
swirling brown leaves, debris, white dust settling on branches,

roof-tops, while at my high window
I stand and wait, rust glazing the horizon.

What I expect is unclear—a resolution,
a beginning, daylight slithering into night,

hearing without sound Sadhana singing Kabir's Bhajan,
"Ghat by ghat birds speak, Master, only of you,

Boatsman, Gardener, Holder of the Scale,
Dandi, God-servant to the Sun."

Birds glide on the back of the wind from ghat to ghat,
singing only of you, Storm,

the Hunter and the Hunted both call your name.

Morning Yoga

The yoga ladies gather at daybreak,
drag plastic chairs over cracked earth
into straggling rows.

Bright greetings and murmured joys
flit lightly through the clustered groups,
conspire against the teacher's drone:

"Bring silence to your practice,
breathe deeply—inhale, sustain, and exhale—
listen to the sacred sound of Ommm . . ."

But the yoga ladies gather to gossip,
exchange the tremors of the day,
and for a while, forget their household chores.

Bougainvillea crowds the opposite shore.
Lotus flowers clog the green water of the canal.
The yoga ladies settle their saris and breathe.

Karimpur

A goat crosses the path leisurely,
followed by a small girl.

Two cows in a side yard munch hay.
A lone horse grazes in the field.

The smell of animals comes in waves.
Birds clamor and sing, shriek at times.

From the rooftop the river gleams
and dinghies reach through green debris.

Electric saws and drills screech.
Scooters scurry from store to tin-roofed store.

Karimpur hums with industry.

The Opposite of Telescope

Again the strange light calls out a name:
it is not starlight,
but reflections from streetlamps,
every other one aflame—
the curved mirror observing not distant objects through emissions
but internal machinations, radiation turned inwards.

Beneath the prim pressed suits and tailored slacks,
beneath the formal smile—
an accent neither here nor there
but either nowhere or everywhere at once—
the glass lenses refracting both sight and sound,
a twist in its terrestrial application.

They are strangers in a strange place,
fishermen casting empty nets
on dry land,
singers singing without a voice.

What do they know of how it feels?

To be beneath the magnifying glass,
two convex lenses,
the dot under observation,
the focus of visible light?

How could they tell if they knew?

When she wears a sari, jhumkas,
kajol around the eyes,
bangles on wrists,
a flower behind the ear,
holding long hair in place—*how exotic and lovely!*

Is that really six yards of silk just wrapped,
not sewn?
Is it always 22 carat gold?

How does it feel?

What does it take to name it?

To be in a place
but not of it,
with it,
but still without,
torn from one life
but still in it,
the scent and sound of it everywhere,
furious, bewildering,

looking into another life from an inside-out telescope.

Along the Canal

The rain tree winds its way up,
black lines silhouetted against a sky
muted and fuzzy with smog.

Beneath its shade the Bojra restaurant bustles,
serves breakfast to morning walkers:
feather-light parathas and fried eggs for a pittance.

Tiny cups of tea, fragrant with spices,
served after the meal, a reverse aperitif,
a bracing send-off to office or home.

The bridge over the canal ends in a puddle.
Wild dogs lie curled in the dust,
well-fed on rats and street waste.

Beyond, rows of market-wallahs
spread wicker baskets of glorious fish,
fresh vegetables glistening in the pale sun.

Portent

Another year comes to an end,
a murder of crows skirl over treetops on my street,
their caws a cacophony of songs
mourning the passing of days.

"*Toba! Toba!* This is an omen of death,"
my grandmother would have said.
"Be still, and pray
the crows don't stray into our yard."

My grandmother is now dead,
the crows still cry out their prophecies,
the days continue to pass
as I grow into my grandmother's face.

Dancing

I want to dance
as if I were alone
the way one moves in a mirror
because it is forgiving.

I never actually learned,
because Bhodrolok do not send their daughters to dancing school.
"What are you thinking!
Imagine if the neighbors knew!"

If I could only dance the way I imagine it,
where my hands and hips move to music only I can hear,
notes writhing like memory,
as if my dreams came true,
as if my life depended on it,

I can hear the syncopation of drums—
tabla-tops thrumming,
sarod wailing—
some singer's deep voice claiming my moves,
directing a dance beyond my control,

I want to dance like the whirling Dervish,
coat flaring wide,
topee askew,
moving to an ecstatic Sufi song,
twirling and twirling to salvation,
oblivion, to the One True Being,

I want to dance like Shiva in a wheel of fire,
multi-armed and multi-hued,
singed by flames,
unhinged by rapture,
the wheel of the universe careening to disaster,

while eyes in the mirror scry moving shadows,
derelict, dangerous, delectable.

Chrysolite

I can feel bruises blooming beneath my skin,
desert flowers in spring, greenish-gold, dragon stone,
somatic memory flickering.

There was a reason for these purple stains—
the aftermath of all the terrible things
we wish that we could change.

Breathing into color the body remains
thin flint sparking now and then
into the remnants of a fire doused in rain.

Can it dispel the terrors of night,
control demons and the wind,
give us the power to scry history yet to come?

Some days we rewrite the script
to say what we wish had been the case—
Take two or twenty-seven if that's what it takes.

Some days we fake a smile,
snap the string tying us to the stake,
and bring it to the brink.

Through the gray shadows of windowpanes,
behind screens we make to hide what should not be seen,
I dream of peridot, green olivine.

Again with green as if it had not already been
written about before and too much—
poets have such limited schemes.

Finding the Center

I pull apart a daisy and weep
for what was known and lost,
but grief should be saved for the truer loss
of that which is unknown and unknowable.

Boring a hole in nightly dreams,
keeping an intentional distance
between the hyacinths which droop
and the child who dreams them endlessly.

As if repetition could make right
the scorched echo of a past not remembered,
the central crime a mystery the elegant detective
will not solve, the trauma unresolved.

The pages of the book shuttered like paradise
for those not brave enough to face the light
or those who just prefer
the shelter of the dark, forgiving earth.

Colors

Life in all its dangerous sweet shapes
is preening colors I have never seen;
these shades are raw, unsafe—their mute spillage
witness to the clamorousness of being.

They creep up in random streaks,
as if Matisse had flung his palette up
to paint the air in vivid strokes of green,
cobalt blue, maddening deep thrusts of pink.

My eyes are singed by hues I barely see;
they hurt; they draw my blood in drips and spurts,
their sudden blaze flares up, then dims,
as forceful in its calm as in its heat.

Life is showing me its tints alright.
I am reeling from the sight.

River at Night

Even at night
the river uncoils from its source
like smoke, like stone,
a song unfolding from first notes.

How to name this flow which has no form,
no definition,
this promise
of continuous change, always the same,
can we believe what we perceive?

Is this a mirage,
ignis fatuus,
the way Rudra, the rough god,
declares the wild heart admits no word,

the way incense curls upward,
delicate, ephemeral,
a tenuous link between temporal things and divinity,

the way Draupadi's sari unfurls,
unfolding endlessly,
a river of silk, uncoiling?

II. The Properties of Time

"What will you do, when it is your turn
in the field with the god?"
      —Louise Gluck

Horology

The quality of light shapes
the contours of a face, a monument,
the ways trees remake the landscape,

the way the day descends
in elliptical turns, the slow churn of hours,
metal casting moving shadows on stone.

Whoever perches on the pedestal preening his quill,
learns the laurel wreath is the other side
of the shield where the other is laid out.

The sun tinkers with silence,
gives up its will to shape the earth,
a leaf spirals in the wind, out of reach.

Inkling

I.

Before the ice came
there was a thaw.
I wondered who would walk in this garden now
all soggy and smashed,
layers of old snow piled, melted,
then drifting high again.

Rose bushes drenched and heavy.
The coming ice would surely kill them.
Bare forsythia branches drag on the ground,
rhododendrons unrecognizable.

Who would sit on this wet stone bench,
watch for the falcon swooping down to snatch prey
mid-air, a feathered fighter jet?

> *The peregrine only hunts birds in flight,*
> *plummeting 200 miles per hour, or more—*
> *owls, hawks, accipitres are not so finicky*
> *and may catch whatever is at hand—*
> *a rabbit, vole, rat, even cat, small dog.*

II

Before ice there was a thought of snow, fire,
crackling wood, smoke on the grate,
although the soaked logs stacked
like so many Swiss soldiers on parade
against the garden shed
would not light up today.

What if snowfall is just a metaphor?
A way of seeing time move in space,
the way starlight reaches us millennia after
the stars have blazed, burnt out their lives?

> *Bernardinelli-Bernstein is hurtling toward our home star—*
> *something big, something unimaginably old, unimaginably cold,*
> *a massive iceball dragging a huge, hazy tail behind it . . .*

III.

Sitting on that wet bench I remember
my sister's small face crumpling into tears,
hands outstretched to a propeller plane,
straining against Khalamma's restraining arms.

Amma was off to New Zealand on a Ford Foundation fellowship,
we were left in the care of Aunt, Uncle, Grandmother.

That year dragged on—an eternity.
At three I learned to be good,
strong for my baby sister's sake.

I held her chubby hands,
helped her walk.
Or am I imagining this from a photograph
found when we cleared out my mother's house?
This faded paper flew to Auckland and back—
it could be the author of my memories.

Why recall that heat and inarticulate grief now,
in the middle of ice and snow?

Today that baby is an astrophysicist,
studies stars and perhaps an errant comet or two.

IV.

Last July was hot, and the garden glorious:
blue hydrangeas, red hibiscus,
many-colored dahlias,
bordered by delicate violet rows of phlox.

In a stone box by the empty stone bench,
new-planted fig trees interspersed with exotic ferns
(the landscaper really outdid himself).

> *Note to the caterer: white tent, tables laid out with*
> *wedding linen,*
> *your china, silver,*
> *an impressive array of crystal stemware,*
> *centerpieces of cut flowers, candles.*

On the patio above, a flower-draped bower,
and a thousand red paper cranes
facing two sets of Chiavari chairs
arranged in regimental rows:
a wide aisle in the middle where
my daughter danced lightly down in white dress and veil.

Why should mothers cry when their child is choking with joy?
I could only pray she would grip this bliss not just that day,
but every day, and every night,
the rest of her impossibly long and tediously happy life.

Now *that* would be worth 18 hours of labor.

V.

But now the snow-dressed bench is stone cold,
my clothes shrink,
and I think of fires in grates and other faces,
other places.

Places I have been and places I still want to go,
places I have seen only in my dreams,
which perhaps do not even exist.

Assuming there is time, which seems to blink
and when I look it's spent,
I don't remember being in it,
or have an inkling where it went.

Properties of Time

The past is unknowable,
blacker than military black, unseeable,
things that happened slide into this dark,
things that did not happen seem real,
things that might have happened slip in between.

Only the present can be true—
the air between us glittering with voices
heard and unheard.

The future is clear and cold.

Properties of the Number Nineteen

What if Nineteen tells no story,
prefigures nothing?

What if it has no historic implacability,
no forward motion?

It is an odd number—
not odd as in not even,
but peculiar, unexpected.

It is a prime number divisible only by itself and one.

Every nineteen years the moon will appear in the same position
among the stars—the Metonic cycle.

The lunar and solar cycles coincide every nineteen years.

It is the beginning and the end of single digits.

It is Kuan Yin, goddess of mercy.

It is *Wahid,* the one, one of the 99 names of God.

There are nineteen angels guarding the gates of Muslim Hell—

which seems odd—who would be trying to break into Hell?
Or is it to keep the residents from getting out?

It is the number of units of time—
days, hours, weeks, years—
revolutions of the wheel,
trees, birds, things which can be counted.

I count them as I can.

Whatever it is I count, the worry starts at eighteen,
because,
inexorably,
Nineteen will be next, and then I wonder,
why now?

Why does Nineteen haunt my days?
Keep me up at night?

Why does it hang around my house—
lurking in the alleyway
there, behind the hydrangeas—
a long-unwanted guest
who will not take the hint to go?

A Rumor of Blue

I want to be wooed with words tinged with blue,
rumors of jazz, and skies, and falling rain,
doors that open wide, birds that never sing.

I want to be where I was before the river ends,
when life was simple, lambent, plain,
when wild and unexpected moments never came.

What if it's true that time's a relative thing?
What happens now, and then, and still to come,
are mutable and fluid—shifts in the wind.

Could we be here and then, together, all at once?
Could we be what we were, and still what is to come?
Are blue and rain, bird and river, one and the same?

Rose

I miss the scent of roses.

These days pink blooms flourish in my neighbor's front yard,
but no smell hangs in the air around them.

When I stroll by on my evening walks,
when I pass by them again and again,
longing for a flicker of past perfume,

even when I thrust my nose deep into the petals,
recklessly braving bees and bugs and thorns,
no whiff of rose, no fragrant waft comes back.

Is the curve of the petal curling around the stigma sufficient
    evidence?

Turning Point

Dust rises like columns of salt
seen from the prophet's backward eye,
revolving to some end not foretold—
the delicate vocabulary of day crumbles.

History is not yet done,
the players are still upon the stage,
the dancers are not sure of the tune,
hurtling to the brink of truth.

Today can never come again,
yesterday's story has not been told—
children who have not yet been born
are asking questions we don't want to know.

Backward Look

That is how it was:
thin air tearing the dark room,
shimmering, saltwater flowing freely—

the claustrophobic curve of the cave
turned inward and down
into a jagged road cluttered with debris,

three days and nights,
though time was androgynous in that space,
lit with the passage of things unseen.

Coffee Mugs

The one with *VC* entwined faded, back when
Vassar was still a girls' school,
not co-ed, and not a Women's College,

one with family photos from a vacation in the Poconos,
made by my ex-sister-in-law whose talent for preserving memories
was not enough to save her marriage.

Then my children's schools, big birthdays,
an elegant black & gold rimmed mug for the Steelers,
one from every job I've ever held.

Soon there will be a "Happy Retirement" mug,
then one from an assisted living facility, possibly a hospice—
do funeral homes give out mugs as "Viewing" favors?

Who needs poems dancing around the stages of my life,
shuffling meaning like a pack of cards,
pulling prophecies from Tarot or advice from an Oracle deck?

Future archaeologists will piece together
everything I've ever been, or thought, or felt,
from shards of coffee mugs teased from excavated dirt.

Walking in the Homewood Cemetery

The dead are still.
They lie in rows
marked by stones:

Hargreave, Coleander, Miraux—
an eclectic mix
except for the Greek lot on the hill

and the Chinese section,
created in 1901,
with stones etched in *hanzi*.

Do the dead care
where they rest?
Among their own laid breast to breast

or strewn through these grounds
wherever a green spot grows
in a shade tree's ruin?

I walk among the dead,
restless.

Rails to Trails

Riders wheel along the river
leaving the libidinous world behind,

past what used to be smokestacks,
past gray eddies and green sludge,

the trail level, meandering,
trees trimmed on both sides,

from here to wherever the wheels roll,
downtown, out of town, whatever town emerges,

> *Cyclists can start in Coraopolis, McMurray, or*
>   *McKeesport,*
> *on the Montour Trail to the Great Allegheny Passage,*

> *over valleys, around mountains,*
> *skirting the Casselman, Youghiogheny, and Monongahela,*

> *then Laurel Highlands to*
> *the Cumberland Narrows,*

through rail tunnels
over viaducts

past dams and monuments
the riders do not pause to look,

moving through time, from Devonian rock formations
to new growth rocks,

the texture of their days
a haze of blue motion,

the fixture of their minds
a destination,

the sky a distant blur,
rising from the trail blue flame,

crossing the continental divide,
then past the Antietam Battlefield,

September seventeenth, 1862,
the killing field, 23,000 casualties,

the bloodiest day of the Civil War so far,
so gory the road's name changed to Bloody Lane—

do ghosts in gray and blue file through these branches,
whispering in the riders' ears?

the scent of trees, grass,
red and white trillium, toothworts, wild ginger, blue phlox,

the sound of wind,
traffic disappears,

voices in the passing towns grow still,
thirst persists,

and all the way the rivers crawl
ever southward, ever winding,

the selvedge of the trail,
while riders swarm the edge,

crunch of tires on limestone,
hum of chain on sprockets,

>   *the trail refuses no rider,*
>   *the sky turns back no cloud,*
>   *the canal asks: what do they know of loss?*

a verdaille scene repeated
for three hundred and thirty-three miles,

the dusk-demented towns house

>   *those who sleep, troubled by dreams,*
>   *those who sing, restless,*
>   *they all wear garlands carved from wooden planks—*

the riders do not care,

their bare glistening shoulders hunched low over handlebars,
their muscled legs urging the wheels to fly—

if time were really on our side,
we would be there, already.

Sports Day

The maypole at the center of the field
is wrapped in streamers and balloons.

Five flagpoles stand beside—
Country, Olympics, Girl Scouts, Girl Guides, and School.

Tri-colored paper hangs on ropes on four sides,
and a wide white circle marks the spot.

Girls in uniforms compete—hijabs cast off for sports.

Bolinas

Twisted trees turn east
as if the rising sun could save them from the wind.
Eucalyptus, cypress, give up this dream.
Even the Sun is a traveler by day,
following the shadows of stars,
memories of a dark breeze.

The shack at the foot of the hill leans out
over restless rocks,
gray planks stir and creak but do not bend
to the unending sound of wind and sea.
Waves creep, then crash on shore,
their voices soar, then dip, and roar again.

Young lovers stand on the porch at the edge of sea and sky,
fierce and gentle, pledging their future lives.

Kennywood Days

Fresh-squeezed lemonade and the Log Jammer,
the slow ride up rickety tracks,
past evergreen branches just out of reach,
drops of water that could not wait,
the scent of anticipation,
a few turns to the top of the hill,
a pause,
the hurtling downward rush,
descending,
drenched and breathless.

The pictures never came out quite right.
Someone else's arm over the face I wanted,
someone else's head in the way.

My Mother's Garden

Bougainvillea grows—great red clumps—
in the back of my mother's garden.
Up on the hill, a torrent of color,
a blaze above the fruit trees.

Pear, guava, apricot, and more—
all planted helter-skelter.
Even the avocado tree
she grew from a seed.

She was my premonition and I, her dream.
Between us a tangle of mother-daughterness,
the drift of lives lived in different spaces,
the folds of time sometimes too wide to bridge.

But in her garden, the afternoon sun behind us,
a breeze riffling the surface of the pool,
endless leaves the torment of a lazy gardener,
sometimes we found our place.

Her little shoes still stand by the door,
waiting for feet that will not come.

For Ruth

This braid of sorrow I carry for you
is not all grief,
these tears are not all sad.
They tell stories of your life:
you took me into your reckless heart,
you never met a person you didn't like,
or saw a movie where you didn't cry.

The love you squandered with such abandon,
as if there were no end to that beginning—
it haunts our minds,
it warms these rooms.
These walls call out: Ruth, Ruth, you are not gone,
you are here, in our wood, in our roots,
you fill our eyes, our lives.

By whatever name we choose to call the One,
in whatever shape or form we make our prayer,
you will be there,
resplendent, fair, and full of joy,
beside the Host of Hosts you will be seen,
no simple woman,
but a Queen of Queens.

Dinner at El Vez

We started with guacamole,
  cilantro, lime, onion, jalapeno & cotija cheese
an explosion of sensation on the tongue,

two pitchers of sangria—one red, one white
  didn't even know white existed;
  it wasn't on the menu.

One came in after the others,
hair still damp—
said he'd gone for a run after work.

Don't remember who else was there.
Only the crunch of fresh chips,
the slide of sangria—

Vesey street a mystery in itself—
so near where money moved,
so far from anything else,

followed by ceviches,
then a flurry of tostados:
  tuna, mahi mahi, carnitas, cauliflower my favorite.

Colleagues, clients, co-conspirators
in the hijacked story of my life—
their faces a blur

their voices a riot of color,
flickering with memories half remembered,
inscrutable laughter.

  Did someone order the Pollo Asado?
  The Pescado a la Plancha?

A team-building exercise,
co-workers out to bond over food, booze,
shared stories.

We sat at a mosaic banquette,
uncomfortable chairs,
walls covered in ponchos and native art.

Who would've thought that years later,
I'd remember the fringed poncho,
bright striped bars flashing like strobe lights?

In the blinding black in between
a memory of unspoken words—
what were they again?

When the conversation veered to indices,
the SEC's overreach on reserves,
incurred losses vs. life-of-the-loan,

I ventured a sentence or two,
heard or unheard—
it made no difference.

> *I spent a decade doing such and so,*
> *and another longing for something else.*

We cannot keep even the small things we dream.

How the West was Won

The boys take a car to Atlantic City after work—
the Resorts Casino Hotel—
to play blackjack, baccarat, five-card stud—
drinks and laughter not a hindrance
to counting cards and calculating odds—
the math that came in handy at work an aid in gambling,
winning because they would not lose,

in the morning, more money in their pockets,
they ride back in the same liveried car—
the driver having waited through the dark—
share one electric razor back and forth,
go straight to work on the trading floor
without morning stubble,
starched shirts not too shabby for having been played in all night,

while lower Manhattan stirs, streaked with early light,
the boys settle behind wide double screens,
Bloomberg terminals on the side,
numbers blazing blue and brilliant in startling rows—
sleep as unnecessary as restraint.

Sampsonia at Night

after a watercolor by Peggi Habets

Whatever else may come,
the lamplights' frosted glow
will burn upon this empty street,
trucks parked against the black curb
will never stir
with headlights shining,
their signals will not blink
as if to say: "My turn now,
my turn to skid off this dark frame
into the pink and purple night."

Elsewhere the world may churn,
workers strike, and gunsights aim,
whatever links may form and fail,
this sky will never fade to gray,
this blackness will not yield to light,
these structures will still stand,
windows shut against the cold
of endless night, and dreamless sleep
still fall upon the lavender blue haze
of Sampsonia blooming by night.

Nefertiti's Daughters

I.

Imagine abundant hair, long, shining like obsidian,
braided in intricate folds, rolled into a high bun,
tied with ribbons, alabaster pins,
or crocodile teeth as decorative combs—
hidden in a headdress.

The profile subtle, strong,
cheekbones to slice through ice,
impossibly long neck,
lips incongruously luscious, red,
kohl-rimmed eyes.

II.

Amenhotep IV abandoned his name,
his religion, and his capital at Thebes,
built Amarna in the worship of Aten—
becoming Akhenaton, the first monotheist.

Nefertiti his Great Royal Wife,
in some depictions also co-ruler,
worshipping Aten in the manner of a Pharaoh.

Their portraits show a loving couple,
holding hands,
about to kiss,
cradling their many daughters.

III

Pity the daughters—all six of them—
no iconic statues in their names.

Fading portraits show one sullen and short,
another with black eyes shining with intelligence and malice,
a third with a painted shadow of her mother's look,
one with kohl and thin brows,
one with a stubborn curve to the mouth,
the last with a bitter turn to the cheek.

Meritaten,
    Meketaten,
        Ankhesenamun,
           Setepenre,
                Neferneferure,
                      Neferneferutaten Tasherit.

Did the sisters squabble, as siblings do,
bother their mother for baubles, dresses, and decisions,
support each other in sisterly grace?
Were there factions and cabals,
temporary alignments or permanent friendships?

Why should the much-married Ankhesenamun get so many
   pharaohs?
First Akhetatun—her own father—after Nefertiti's death,
then Tutankhamun, the golden pharaoh,
then an elder courtier, and finally her own maternal grandfather,
   Ay.

Evidently Ankhesenamun tried to evade her fate,
wrote to a Hittite King to marry one of his sons—
any one would do—
this an act of intolerable rebellion.

IV.

Would her sisters be grateful for avoiding this fate?
Did they even have husbands, lovers, unknown to history?
Did they live quietly—content in royal isolation?

Did they look at the light of lost stars
and wonder if there was another way to live?

Did they slink along the alleys of Amarna,
accompanied by slaves,
seeking a hierophant to decipher the lines of their future?

Did they pass on to their daughters
a story of silent revolt,
as they in turn to theirs?

V.

Nefertiti ruled as co-regent—
earlier in the eighteenth dynasty,
Queen Hatshepsut ruled Egypt for 20 years;
her daughter Neferure then took the throne.

Always the wives and daughters
of great men rose.

While legally equal to men,
Egyptian women were not schooled,
but were expected to manage households
not hold other positions.

VI.

Millenia have not changed the rules:
by the turn of the century
the daughters of Nefertiti take to the streets:

"The girls of Egypt are a thin red line—
beyond this we will not go.
It is enough."

VII.

Mainstream media covered male protesters,
except when a woman was raped.

Written out of history,
Women protestors wrote their own stories.

VIII.

Egyptian spring came and went,
Nefertiti's daughters,
black hair hidden in hijabs,
continue protests.

III. Mad Birds and Shadows

"The mad bird makes love to the moon."
—Urdu Ghazal

"The shadow seeks union with the sun
but cannot achieve it.
It is clearly impossible,
yet the shadow thinks of nothing else."
—Attar

Eating a Blood Orange in the Morning

What if I could keep this sweetness all day,
carry it around like a talisman,
rose quartz memory of taste?

Could this be the tether to real things
holding me to earth, solid, mutable,
unable to see beyond?

Perhaps the Archer has gone too far to return,
bring back the blood moon to the beginning,
where we see the other for the first time

with new eyes, wild and undiscovered,
what was hidden before now bared—
signs the stars reveal in parts.

I want to dream of oranges
but find instead dead cardinals littered under trees.

August

Then, when the black nightingale returns to the forest,
when the audacious sun is high,
I wonder, beneath the waves,
where a few more wing beats would have taken me,

when autumn is almost upon us,
and the wheat is high,
apples turn red among the green and golding leaves,
my heart, unwinding, begins its slow descent

into the lion's mouth,
forgetting the unchangeable past,
the years that turn and turn, implacable,
the wheel of fortune, oiled and relentless,

takes me again to the Blue Slide Park,
still echoing with my children's high laughs,
a kestrel bouncing off the horizon,
as-sumut, azimuth, alpha and omega.

Wind from the 45th Floor

This building bites my skin through to the bone.
Some wind it steals from North or South or West.
Some beast it finds to nip at flesh and stone.

Clouds fly past the glass panes of my wall:
some black, some white, some gray crests
of wind-drenched speed, a blue squall

of small birds, debris, what nature brings
downtown, and leaves to swirl the air, unblessed
by curse or prayer, it bites and sings.

Pink Moon

Could it be tonight? The moon's orbit
comes close to earth,

catching us in its path, pink phlox
blossoming among weeds, long grasses—

the hermaphrodite coral spawns each year,
triggered by a new moon—

whatever its arc,
whatever shape it takes,

we are trapped in its pull,
pinned to the ground by gravity.

A billion gametes flood the ocean floor,
an underwater blizzard of color—

lipids rise to the surface,
tiny eggs and sperm scramble to join in time—

synchronicity ensuring survival
for entire colonies of coral reefs.

The amorous moon sheds white light on dark water.

A Hint of Pink

Pink was never so pale as this shade,
This hint of slivered radish on a plate,
Translucent, glowing, a glimmer of flame.

Promises Mailboxes Make

after a black and white photograph by Brian Sesack, 2021

There will be a message.
It is coming fast toward you.

It will be from a friend of the past,
handwritten in purple ink.

Will you forgive them?
Perhaps you are the one who needs to be forgiven.

The universe is manifesting this event—
the mailbox is just a messenger.

It could be a letter from the lottery,
or a bouquet of wildflowers picked just for you.

A thousand paper cranes may appear,
tied with red string.

The shadow side will disappear
and the mailbox glow with incandescent light.

What is visible and not visible blur,
indistinguishable.

Mailboxes make promises they do not keep.
The chariot doesn't come.

Departure

after a painting by David Muenzer, oil on canvas, 2019

Then it was time to go.
She stands there
in the window of the cabin smiling.

Sun-sprinkled stones reflect the vocabulary of light,
but the girl doesn't speak—
her intentions unknown behind an enigmatic stare.

The arc of day declines to night.
Does she miss the bewildering red gaze of the sun?
Does she say goodbye or greet the hours yet to come?

The First Snowfall

The dogs are wild with joy,
they make dog-angels on the white lawn,
drag branches heavy with wet, fall to the ground.

My boots are too short for these drifts.
I throw two red balls to the happy pups,
but this Holiday postcard is not for me.

Dress me in summer, and a hard breeze,
heat crackling through shimmering muslin,
glistening under a torpid sun.

Give me a monsoon rain,
artillery pounding drops,
water hanging like sheets, persistent.

Take me to a winter wind, dusty and dry,
a Harmattan blowing
these silver drifts to smithereens.

Dust

Solitude is all we need to be seen
in the dark telescope of the sky,
split by a million splintering stars
breathing bluer than blue flames.

To live is relearning to be alone—
all else is dream grinding into stone,
curling back to maya—love and illusion both.

If Earth is the common mother of us all,
teaching us to breathe the alien air
as one by one we emerge into the world,
do we miss the lonely water of the womb?

Watching costumed children call "Trick or Treat!"
my daughter cries out: "Oh my ovaries!"
We are each alone in knowing what we need.

Hotter than Hades and all the wild
fires of California, thin prickling under skin,
thick with smoke and longing,
burn me with eyes that rise to fall again,
breathe me into dust,
the swirling cosmos, alone at last.

Day's End

Shadows scale the window-slats in slanted grooves.
A strange sun dips and claws its crimson flight
to darkness, where I also would go if I could.

Linen grass paper lines the walls in sober gray.
A single lamp, unlit, hides the corner table.
Edging out the hesitant light, small shadows creep
and grow to ominous shapes.

There is no aura left, no ardent whiff of life.

Only the end-stench of remnant smoke from dead cigars.
This is the long day's dying breath, caught hold,
resurrected for the moment's slender slot.

I shut the door behind me as I leave.

Nightscape

Left behind, the tautness in my body subsides,
reverberates, a vibration
echoing the arrow's lovely arc in flight.

Then again Amun has not yet parted
the primordial seas, and endless night
awaits the four horsemen,
the sound of hooves and spurs tight in the air

where dark meets dark, black cries greet faintly
the great unknown, and a tingling peace rushes in.

I am on a green hill and field in sunlight,
where shadows have no place; I wander
burning my mind in search of a cool shade
which does not live, and never has, in this valley

of a thousand streams where
daisies turn up their faces,
wild for color and sound.

What Happened

Then again today the sun rose,
the earth turned, the palimpsest
of our lives settled, grew calm,
formed another layer in geologic time,

strata upon strata of meaning,
if one could only decipher the code,
the stories told by stone,
imprints, fossilized remains,

while above, akashic records stretch
across alternative futures,
infinitesimal changes in the present
opening myriad paths—

Syrinx transforming into a thousand hollow reeds,
each reed a pipe,
each pipe a way of calling home,
wailing to the water gods—

as if akash, the sky, could contain
this mystery, this odd return
to old uncertainties—
where were we when we spoke?

First and last things hang between us,
before and behind obscured,
what happened in the interim now lost—
at least, burned into background,

the recesses of the mind, scorched, alone,
naan sticking to the side of a Tandoori oven,
a mad bird reaching for the moon,
a shadow craving union with the sun.

Driving on the PA Turnpike

Dusk, and the Blue Mountain lies in its own light,
soft peaks smudged against the sky,
traversing the unintended day.

I speed along the highway,
road racing beneath me,
tires throb, sparks flying

the way they flew once between us,
when you stood up, and I fell into your eyes,
the color of bright oceans, the unlimiting sky.

Aubade

Like Li Po looking at the moon after rain,
humming, I am awake as dawn
comes crawling over the hard edge of night,

throwing yellow hues over trees
and smokestacks, the Monongahela dark
and winding below the hills,

steel barges filled with coal or grain
gliding down the river through early morning fog,
pulled by towboats.

What were you trying to say?
I should have known there was more
to the words than it seemed,

should have listened to the spaces in between,
silence hovering above,
solitude settles beneath.

Sleep escapes me,
and I dream with open eyes
of a lotus clinging to a stream.

My hand on your belly,
heat seeping through my veins.

Riptide

Midnight dips in Falmouth Bay,
luminescent algae flaming the black sea,
rock edges cutting the soles of my feet,
the coldness of the waves, a salty breeze,
the night sky miming a blazing deep,
and drunken, happy youth, immortal, carefree,
sweet as only memories can be.

Decades disappeared in a blink:
my youth, your birth, the turning of the earth
a round moon bobbing to a steady beat:
two bruised hearts reach out, then panic, and retreat.

If Then

If you say so, these hours stand still,
the rippling day freezes in its frame,
the sky leans down to touch earth
with delicate fingers.

Shoab the beautiful bathes in the ghat,
emerges dripping, wearing a thread-bare lunghi,
builds a fire in the center of the courtyard,
places a black korai over it to heat.

If you say this, there is no rift in time,
al-Khwarizmi would not have birthed the cifr,
making tables to torture children through the ages,
Fibonacci could not have drawn the spiral galaxies,

Durga's many arms would still wave,
the resplendent Greeks, loving logic,
would have failed to probe the future,
and the mysteries of probability would be dark.

Memory

Recalling your stride,
I unlace longing like bedeviled stars,
unfurl silver hair—
floating clouds on your countenance,
dream seahorses, tulips, seaweeds writhing
green and unguent,
underwater worms
becoming other creatures.

Only the past is real, a paso doble watching
for hints of flinches, half-forgotten winks,
whoever holds the needle stitching the world together,
this summer's day unfolds in slow motion,
waiting for the warm and fragrant night.

Breakable Things

For a clumsy person,
life is full of accidents, waiting.

Glasses in my hands have a short life expectancy,
porcelain statues I never dust.

Bones kept like the best linen—
never used daily for basketball or skiing.

Promises are hard to keep,
hearts crack when jostled roughly.

Beguiled

I saw a boy standing in the sun
without his shirt,
short shorts,
bare legs and chest dazzled the sod
like some bloody Greek God.

What was his goal?

Just burn some eyes
and bother the dreams of sober women—
wives, mothers, and friends,
whose gentle lives
unfold in predictable ways
of making beds, breakfasts, appointments,

deadlines, and yet—

the thought of making you
quickened some breaths that day.

Nights

when the arc of the mind is taut
with possibilities, when the dour moods
of day soften to cricket sounds,
nightbirds singing to stars,

when the heart is bare, uncovered,
exposed for the renegade it is,
the shields of habit shed for the dark,
when the hum of the household dims,

then, Love, you stretch out on my mind
like the movement of leaves listening
to the moon's truculent cries
as it leans to the task,

fulfilling the sundry dark purposes of night.

After Rilke

We are mute in the face of longing.
The body's breath, held still,
is a blue death
repeated each day,
each hour,
maimed minutes,
trampled in passing,
mortal, eclectic—
the rigors of what is right,
or not,
the severity of the test
testament to its own will—
some blitzkrieg of the night,
this silence.

The Globe

of the world seems small these days.
It sits on my desk, multi-colored, curious,
the seas deep-hued, mysterious,
hills and mountains raised.

All it takes to spin it is a touch—
I turn and turn the circling sphere,
a bubble revolving here and there
in great uncertain swoops I rush

to chronicle the things I dare—
some brown shape keeps coming through
to taunt the blue-edged ribbons' curlicues
around deep swirls of text.

There is not space enough for me and you
in this world, or the next.

Beaches

I never walk on rocky beaches
but stones like blunt blades
make etchings on my feet.

And you, which beaches do you glide on now?
Which sands stretch out
a soft tapestry of powdery shoals?

Which reach of land unfurls
a spectacle of glinting reefs,
mollescent, sheer and quiet

as waves which lick the lips
of beaches like flat globes—
a Gulistan for lovers to slip into?

That is the difference between me and you.
Pebbles spring like weeds wherever I go—
your toes are touched by air alone.

Properties of Green

I.

Sequence is not linear
in the way I see green,
so it is not the first time I remember,

but anticipation,
when the blush of new buds break,
when black branches begin to bloom,

not unlike love,
where the first time turns to gray,
and the next and the next fade away.

II.

Is green to be believed as we perceive it,
not merely as molecules and radiant energy,
but as essential ingredients in nature?

Whitehead says this perception is limited
by our current understanding of natural laws,
we cannot know what green is capable of

in other epochs of the universe,
when other laws of nature are reigning,
because we have not yet imagined them.

III.

It is the color of Islam—
respect, submission, serenity,
and the Holy Prophet (May peace be upon him!),
who conquered half the known world
under the green flag,
so it is also the color of conquest.

IV.

Green is the color of money—
prosperity, materialism, possibly greed,
although we could argue this is a stretch.

Progressives have also claimed the color—
climate change, renewable energy, eco-consciousness,
all facets of the health of the planet.

Odd that they agree
on the power of green to make whole
the objects of desire.

V.

Shakespeare called green the color of envy,
corroding friendship,
even love careening to destruction.

Desire is a thing we dream,
could die for,
dissolving into the greener than green Other.

VI.

Tree pythons can have green eyes,
and cats—the Chinchilla long-haired Persian,
the Abyssinian, and some Tabbies.

Fewer than 2% of humans have green eyes—
startling when you stumble across them,
impossible to forget.

One girl's green eyes mesmerized the world
30 years ago, and again recently on the cover of Life—
she had aged under the Taliban.

VII.

Researchers say
green can improve reading ability in the young
and the illiterate.

As when Jibril appeared in the Cave of Hira
to the illiterate camel-driver,
commanded: "Read!" and he read.

VIII.

It is the color between yellow and blue
on the visible spectrum—
it has a thousand names:

celadon, emerald, lime,
viridescent, aquamarine,
a variation of cyan . . .

Green is the loop I am in
when I remember
what might have been.

Absence alone cannot save us from Eros.

After Cataracts

I.

Color came back first,
sharp, glowing, bursting like a storm.

I had forgotten how it could be—
shades an echo in my memory,

a host of things seen and remembered,
confusingly appealing, but hazy,

like a scent once known
in the irretrievable past.

II.

I imagine Eve opened her eyes
to a world molten with color,

just so, drowning in senses,
the fronds of first ferns a blistering green,

the sky unknowable azure,
before clouds, rain,

before the first flower,
before comprehension.

III.

When things which were not seen
are visible again, can scent come back?

My nose to your pulse,
counting the number of times the heart beats per minute,

the memory of pheromones faint,
but there,

as if the mind has a cache at the back,
unknown to the frontal cortex.

IV.

Can taste come back? Like a madeleine
triggering history, the past a palette unfolding in color—

sweet, sour, salty,
savory of all kinds,

the tongue has its own predilections,
twists to its own rhythms,

the impulse to return
to its addictions.

V.

Then there is touch—fingers recall the feel
of silk, the softness of soft things,

the hardness of hard, and yet, tactile senses fade
like others, muting with age to a middle range,

pain the other side of touch—the body remembers
contractions, the cervix expanding,

but that is lost in the joy after,
the incomparable newborn scent.

VI.

Can one hear again sounds never heard before?

The Red Thread

        stretches/twists/breaks/snaps/curdles/
fades like a Bindi after bathing

or Mehndi after days.

How did the thread wear out, dissolve?

I am on the carousel of submission,
whiplashed from one to another, deciphering
the self from the other.

Can stitches be repaired? Like a
good wool sweater worn at the elbows

or a marriage frayed at the edges?

Ariadne's thread rope-walking
through the Labyrinth *to,* and not *from,*
the Monster.

    Ariadne is also Arachne, who devours
    her mate, weaver of a web which is herself.

The foible of string unwinding,
a gift the fates have stitched and unstitched.

    A single track, coiled, recoiled, on itself.

The ulnar artery connects the ring finger
to the heart.

The Kalava ties one to another for all time—
so many reincarnations.

The crane dance performed at Delos
and Mount Fuji, intricate, deliberate.

The Kimono ceremony and *Gai Halud*—
lit up with red.

> *Who can lust after eternity when the ring*
> *of recurrence spells a spiral,*

coil shaped, infinite line,
the endless loop of a mobius strip?

> *What is knotted/repeats/doubles/broken/fantastical?*

All tropes overlap—
the language of narration is borrowed,
stuttering and inarticulate.

The red thread leads everywhere, both
inside and out of the Labyrinth.

What is not God is imperfect.

Shall we go again?

Notes and Asides

Bhajan is a devotional song or prayer. Kabir's poetry is primarily in the form of *Bhajan*.

The quotation is from Nabaneeta Dev Sen, a Bengali writer who wrote prose in English, but poetry mostly in Bangla, from her collection, *Acrobat,* translated by her daughter, Nandana Dev Sen. Nabaneeta Dev Sen wrote in "Bangla because it was a political choice" to reject the colonizers' language, but also because she was deeply worried about the future of regional languages and literature with the growing ubiquity of English. However, Dev Sen had a "fraught" relationship with language and wrote some poems in English that she said she couldn't write in Bangla.

For me Eve's emergence into the "red confusion of words" is not just her loss of innocence in biblical terms. It also prefigures the centuries of male gaze afterwards, the notions of "menstruation" as somehow tainted, of evil, and of female seduction (the scarlet woman) vs. the issue of male desire.

Ghat is a Bengali word for the wide stone steps leading from the banks of the river down to the water's edge—part dock, part pier, and part meeting place for the village—where women wash their laundry, and villagers bathe, congregate.

Karimpur is a village in the Narsingdi District of Bangladesh where my mother was born. My mother built a high school for girls in Karimpur in 2003 to mitigate the local practice of pulling girls from the (free but co-ed) public schools after sixth form in order to marry them off. My sister and I have kept up the school after her death in 2016. We are now struggling with the resurgence of a very conservative Islamic movement which has required our 600 or so students to wear hijabs during school, which they take off only for sports activities.

Draupadi is a heroine in the Hindu epic, *Mahabharata*. She is married to the five Pandava brothers. When one of them loses her in a dice game, Dushasana drags her by the hair to the court and attempts to remove her clothing in public. Miraculously her sari never ends, and she is spared this humiliation.

Some of the language in the last stanza of "Properties of the Number Nineteen" was suggested by my friend and fellow-poet Timons Esaias.

Bernardinelli-Bernstein is one of the largest comets ever recorded with an estimated nucleus of about 93 miles (150 kilometers) wide. This comet takes millions of years to circle the sun and will make its closest approach to earth on January 21, 2031, when it will be within a billion miles of the sun. It is visible now and will likely remain visible through the 2040s.

The line "rising from the trail blue flame" in "Rails to Trails" was inspired by some language in the poem "Velocity," written by my friend and fellow-poet, Alyssa Sineni.

I wrote "Bolinas" for my daughter Maya and her husband, Kinori, on the occasion of their engagement in Bolinas.

Kennywood Amusement Park opened in my other home of Pittsburgh, Pa. in 1898. Today it continues the tradition of wooden roller coasters and other old-fashioned rides, as well as newer high-speed steel gauntlets, providing "clean family fun." The Log Jammer was one of my favorite water rides which unfortunately has been discontinued. I say: "Bring it back!"

I first heard the story of a mad bird in love with the moon as a child in an Urdu ghazal, but both the mad bird and the shadow craving union with the sun were images likely taken originally from Farid-Ud-Din Attar's *Conference of the Birds,* which I read much later in the translation by Sholeh Wolpe.

Cifr in Arabic translates today to "cipher." It came from *sunya,* the centerpiece of the Hindu-Arabic mathematical system, which means zero. "Cipher" means empty, referring to the empty column in the abacus. The invention of *sunya* or *cifr* made many other mathematical constructs and inventions possible.

I borrowed "unlace longing" from a poem by Forough Farrokhzad as translated by Sholeh Wolpe.

In "Properties of Green," I adapted a phrase from Leila Chatti's poem "After Touching you, I think of Narcissus Drowning," and of course, "greener than green" is stolen from Sappho's "greener than grass," as translated by Anne Carson in *If Not, Winter.*

"The Red Thread" is a one-sided conversation with J. Hillis Miller's "Ariadne's Thread: Repetition and the Narrative Line." The italicized sections are paraphrased from this article. But in a sense, this poem also summarizes many of the themes in my collection: the binaries of east/west, male/female, divine/profane.

About the Author

Shaheen Dil is a reformed academic, banker, and consultant who now devotes herself to poetry. She was born in Dhaka, Bangladesh and lives in Pittsburgh. Her poems have been widely published in literary journals and anthologies. Her first full-length poetry collection, *Acts of Deference,* was published in 2016 by Fakel Publishing House. Shaheen is a member of several poetry workshops, including The Pittsburgh Poetry Exchange, the DVP/US1 Poets, and the Porch Poets. She received her undergraduate degree from Vassar College, a master's degree from Johns Hopkins University, and a Ph.D. from Princeton University.

www.ingramcontent.com/pod-product-compliance
Lightning Source LLC
Chambersburg PA
CBHW072050160426
43197CB00014B/2699